DESTROYER OF MAN

Destroyer of Man

Selected Poems
Dominic Owen Mallary
1984-2008

Black Ocean
Boston - New York - Chicago

Black Ocean
P.O. Box 52030
Boston, MA 02205
blackocean.org

Cover design by Homeless Media

ISBN 978-0-9844752-1-6

Library of Congress Cataloging-in-Publication Data

Mallary, Dominic Owen, 1984-2008.
  Destroyer of man : selected poems / Dominic Owen Mallary. -- 1st ed.
    p. cm.
  ISBN 978-0-9844752-1-6 (alk. paper)
  I. Title.
  PS3613.A4526D47 2011
  811'.6--dc22
                                2010047067

Printed in Canada

FIRST EDITION

CONTENTS

FOREWORD
by Janaka Stucky

INTRODUCTION
by Cosmo Kilburn DiGiulio & Vincent Milburn

COME UP FROM YOUR COUGH-IN

WACHUSETT

CLOSED FOREVER

FOREWORD

When a colleague at a New York press asked me whether I'd be interested in publishing a posthumous collection of Dominic Mallary's work, I was intrigued—but skeptical. While he had self-published a chapbook before he died in 2008, he was much more well-known for his music as the frontman for the hardcore/punk band Last Lights than for his poetry. That said I felt compelled to at least skim some of his work, which immediately drew me in.

As an aging punk, fellow Emerson alum and Massachusetts native, I felt an early kinship with Dominic as a person. That kinship deepened as I delved further into the immense collection of unpublished work he had left behind. I began recognizing influences from Eliot and Whitman, as well as more radical writers and thinkers like Antonin Artaud and Hakim Bey. After going through almost 200 pages of his work, it became clear to me that a powerful book waited inside there, and I felt it imperative to bring forth the book that Dominic never had the chance to assemble.

While it's impossible to say what a full-length collection might have looked like had Dominic put it together himself, I've worked closely with his friends to select a collection that we feel is both representative and cohesive. The first section of this book, *Come Up From Your Cough-In*, reflects the content of the chapbook that Dominic released in his lifetime—which we decided to leave relatively untouched in regards to order and edits. The second section is a long poem titled, *Wachusett*, whose sequence has been unaltered though we introduced line edits where they seemed appropriate. The third section, *Closed Forever*, is a selection of poems chosen and ordered by myself, Vincent, and Cosmo. Line edits were also made.

In editing the second and third sections of this book, we tried to be as respectful of Dominic's voice as possible. The process had to be intensely thoughtful since we didn't know which poems he might have intended for publication, which were drafts, and which— perhaps—he may have never wanted to see the light of day. At every turn we had to ask ourselves what his intentions were and how his efforts would be perceived by a readership that didn't have the same benefits of friendship or context that we did. Ultimately, what you now find in your hands is our best attempt at honoring a fiercely aware and unapologetically intense poetic voice.

Dominic's particular sensibility as both an academic and an outsider to academia has given me pause to think about the aesthetic zeitgeist of his would-be peers in the world of contemporary American poetry. There is an eloquence to the lack of varnish in this work, and a magnetism reminiscent of Rimbaud emanating from its raw core. Working on it has been transformative for me in a variety of ways. I hope you find it as intriguing, arresting, and unexpectedly beautiful as I do.

INTRODUCTION

Dominic Mallary was a successful musician, an avid artist, a writer and a poet; all the while staying true to a deeply ingrained ethos of punk rock and DIY spirit. This book is just as much a product of that lifestyle as it is the manifestation of a life's work.

Suffering through bouts of insomnia, Dom could often be found up at all hours of the night, feverishly creating a new masterpiece. Rather than relying on others, he consistently released his art on his own terms. In their original form, parts of this book were printed on heavy stock paper at a local copy store near his home in rural Massachusetts, folded, stapled and hand numbered out of 25.

Always the performer, Dom died after a freak accident on stage while leading his band in December of 2008. He was 24.

There has been an enduring interest in Dom's music, including discographies from Think Fast! and Mightier Than Sword Records which have been released world-wide. However those closest to Dominic know that he cherished the beauty of the written word most of all and it is our wish that he be remembered for his romantic, often cynical, but mostly eloquent illustration of the human condition.

After his death, a group of close friends and admirers reprinted and distributed large quantities of this work in the same DIY manner as the original. These poems were known to be some of Dom's favorites, but they are by no means comprehensive. Even at his young age the author had amassed an enormous library of paintings, musical projects and poems, all of which he freely shared and passed among friends. Some still surface occasionally, reclaimed from old notebooks or hard drives. All are prized, respected and admired.

This is a collection of what we believe to be his best work, but they are no longer just poems. They're the embodiment of the potential we lost when we lost Dom.

CKD & VRHM
November, 2010

~

This book would not be possible without the support of the following people. For this we thank you: the Turano & Mallary families, Angela Fallavollita, John Venuti, Janaka Stucky, Rachael Rakes.

Most people waste their youth wishing they were dead and then they waste the rest of their lives wishing they were young again. But I will never end up like that. Wishing I was young instead of dead.

COME UP FROM YOUR COUGH-IN

THE FUTURE NEVER CAME

In the year 2000, the yawning fangs of peace will declare the world over and better for it. Man will be so cool He'll end human suffering with a hard nudge of the jukebox, and it'll be easy listening and sleep aid commercials on the information superhighway to Hell for the next ten thousand years, the jammed cars all burning in place like self-immolating child stars until the oil runs out and everybody goes "Awww!"

In the year 2000, Art and Commerce will sign a cease fire and start sucking each others cocks until kingdom come. The student loan departments will forgive and forget so the Kids can cash-in their MFA degrees and place their bets on the world championship match between the Future and History, hoping for the body count to beat the spread.

In the year 2000, Christ will rise from the dead to feed on the brains of the living. Mystery will surrender unconditionally to Progress, and the last noble savage will leave the jungle for the projects. Dust to dustbuster. Amen.

In the year 2000, we were not left at the altar but in the curled clogs of pubic hair at the bottom of the public record, the conversation between money and itself goes on unabated. White trash, black trash, magenta trash, lavender trash, lemon-lime trash, pre-owned trash, born-again trash, and the invisible trash of the poor. I spent two thousand years prospecting in the strip mine of the soul and all I got was store credit.

The pack-ice is packing.
The gods are consolidating.
Life insurance, white light, white power.

The interstate is a dead end. The earth is a screaming mouth.

This tiny earth is a very large intestine.

ILLITERATURE

The reality cartel has my generation
hung by its eyes: life
lost in parentheses from first light—
        (When you are born
                they set you on fire)
You can spend a lifetime telling people they're right,
cheerleading for the police
and blowing potpourri up the world's well-wiped shitter:
        (w/ everything said sans the truth,
            we retreat into illiterature,
        the old People's Republic of nowhere:
            blood feuds, solar systems,
            world debt, ruins . . .)
        "Man" burns at ninety-eight degrees
and the poets in Hell are beat,
        for in hard times,
            beauty is harder.

THE BAD NEWS

Hegemony is just a word but it's speaking to me
at this party
where the kids are all dead at their drinks.

The skating rink is filled with sympathizers.
The shopping malls are haunted houses
and the haunted houses are sleeper cells.

Girls still laugh in the rain where the cops can't see
but the air is poison
and the newspaper keeps asking me:

Did you get what you paid for?
Is this what you wanted?
Did you get what you paid for?

What tired phrase could I offer
where Heart is so arrested
where Heart is so vacantly throbbing dust?

Hegemony is just a word but it's speaking to me.
The bad news
is written all over your face.

COME UP FROM YOUR COUGH-IN

Reborn, rebubbled. We awoke from a passing week, wake eye
yoke from the family tree. The fruit fell out of the sky. The Lovely
sleep in the dirt. All carless grace comes crawling out of the
naked sea/inner thigh. The apple sings in the gutter: "Up, up,
come up from your cough-in, Lassie! Heaven is fulla snobs.
He'll call in the army of Babylon, blame it on the Adam bombs,
burn Eden into earth, and America will be illuminated too!
So, wake up sister! Wake up brother!
Be at my wake and we'll drink the holywater!"
Now, Cunts run with the moon. Cocks work the rock and die soft,
membering sleep, & I am left building an ark out of paper bags.
King James Underground blowing up bloodbanks. Crawl up
on ye Cross and pay the rent! The mystery drags on... capitalist
& communist. There is no eye in sea. Reborn, rebubbled, reborn.

SUPERMARKET

Starving. www.Sarah and the Jihadist. Enter.
The Supermarket (trademarked,
pasteurized blood from stone) 4 food. No body eva.
Wonders. About where dis Superabundance.
Comes from. Besides something about.
The Greatest Con-Try in the World. Sarah says.
Holding flesh-amputated-from-the-machine-which-mothered-it.
In her Hands. Blasphemy, says Jihad. World war
peace. The fucked and. The fucking. Making the Unspoken
Link between his Nuts, his Heart and
His Politics. Spoken.

WET FLOOR. Car bomb. AC is eating us up.
This hungry page cannot be displayed. In
The Supermaket the facts are Mystical. Pray.
Frozen altar. Mass accumulation of garbage.
In Complete Ctrl. Starving Jihadist stabs www.Sarah.
Through the Sssshrinkwrapped PaprHrt screaming
"DELETE DELETE DELETE" Puking blood.
In the Wet Aisle. Lost in the freon stars.
Sarah: Ohmyfuckinggod
(laughing out loud)

NEW YORK TIMES

The newspaper is a suicide
note.

Depression writes
the laws.

THE YANKEE BOOK OF THE DEAD

I will write nonsense
I will write nothing for the good people
in the Yankee Book of The Dead

I was raised
where open mouths dribble church on rocky roads
and nothing grows

where ghosts spend the century
prank calling girls
who'll drown in swimming pools the following summer

Lonely us in the backyard building crosses for kittens
Lone world in the darkness
come to not

Where the dog digs for bone
and beats his nose to the dirt
like he's housecalling hell

White eyes leering at the world-skin
underneath the lawn
where the shit stews in tongues

and the June rain jigs
horny for the sea
while the traffic weeps light

MY NEIGHBORHOOD

My neighborhood is forty feet tall and red all over.

After school, the children run around and stab each other with letter-openers screaming "Jew!" or "A-rab!" and sometimes they fall in real love too, and everything is fun and games until someone gets hurt.

At home, old men snap the paper and read between the lines because that's where the sex is.

My mother is a driveway paved last spring for basketball and street hockey practice.

My dad is a deed to the house and he's laughing because the mortgage has a joke to tell him and everyone's in on it.

Nothing has ever been in my neighborhood.

It's holding steady on the reality index somewhere between "Way out there!" and "A little bit creepy . . ."

Every evening, the fathers perch themselves on their front porches and with their finest steak knives they cut out a piece of their heart and hold it sadly towards the sun which is saying "So long, suckers" to another day.

The piece of heart no longer beats in its home; rather, it beats with the other homeless pieces of heart.

Finally, when the blood slips out of it, like jelly slips from the mouth of a very serious man, it is only several thousand less blood cells that could potentially develop into chronic lymphocytic leukemia.

Meanwhile, in another part of the galaxy, the news is selling me the future, and everything is looking like it's going to hell in a handbasket, or "Just fine," as my mother would say.

In my neighborhood, the glaciers aren't dying, they've gone underground, where they lurch through the sewers like mythic alligators living on the flesh of the stray dogs or marijuana addicts.

Twice, I have seen Santa Claus, and one time he told me to always ask who benefits from human suffering.

"Follow the cookie trail," he muttered through his frosty beard, "Ho! Ho! Ho!"

The second time, Santa said nothing and offered me and my sister only a handshake full of broken fingers.

We took his hands in ours and squeezed just to be sure Santa knew there's no such thing as a free lunch.

From that point on, he understood our mutually beneficial relationship.

In the winter sometimes, it will snow for days and I will sit by the window with my sister while the elderly suffocate in their luxury cars.

When they find them, the dead almost always smell like a bad conscience.

In my neighborhood, the lab rats go to heaven with the humans.

"What's the big idea?" they ask the Lord and He laughs a hearty laugh and the lab rats laugh too but the people don't—they wonder why it's so hot up here and they go looking for the thermostat.

Most nights, back on Earth, I lie under the power-lines and watch the lights go out, one by one, just as dusk becomes darkness and nobody wants to know anything in my neighborhood.

There, I think about where the power lies while the wires sigh and everyone is choking to death on the thick middle of their lives and I laugh as well because if the oil is running out, someone had better go and catch it.

I even believe in Christ sometimes
like when the bug lantern lights up with doom
and the insects get what's coming to them.

Other times, I just scream "Cannibal!" over and over again:
on a Sunday morning, in the supermarket, between dreams, under abandoned cars as the circular dead end of the road...
There, I scream "Cannibal" at the sky and wait for lightning bolts or bad credit or none of the above.

And that's what we do in our neighborhood.

I eat the raw flesh of my neighbors and laugh with my mouth full, the blood slopping down my chin to the asphalt, over the discarded bones, and under the sewer grates where it collects in bloody icicles on the cold skin of the glaciers.

Over time, these frozen rivers have taken on the black-red ideology of by-gone "liberation" movements and anarcho-primitivist
        pamphleteers.

Tomorrow, and the day after, there will be treasonous
rivers of ice in the sewers.

They are plotting against us but they don't know who controls
the shitters in my neighborhood.

SONG OF SCAMS

End
Out of time:
night buys-out dawn, the know-nothing dark floods
with fluorescent light: an empire shakes
off its blues and sings:

"Murderers of the future, unite!"

You cannot believe the fury of swindled thieves:
it's apple pie-hot, tongue-scalding
shit of the mouth: Song of the Extended Clearance Sale:
Song of the Inverted Desire:
                    swan song of the sedated hogs
                            at the Last Supper of King Swine:

the original o.g.
From the Author of the redundant American Dream:
                    el persuito de la happiness:
The Song of Scams:

Last Saturday, late evening:
I was barely-there, naturally, when I ran into myself
wandering the desert for another beer in the deaf dark
Party of God: I awkwardly embraced myself and we made small
talk over the smudged faces of the doomed kids, saying:
"Poets today are just dying for you to know how smart everyone
tells them they are," I sneered and replied,
"Fuck this," (the search bearing no fruit thus far) and I said,
"They're just the nerds who spent high school sucking the teacher's
asshole. They have nothing to say about the mutually-assured
destruction of Today."

The cold grail captured, I trailed off,
"The Superego must be slain in order to be reborn as . . ."

holy ghost: pillar of salt. Sales pitch, zoning law.
The geography of inner space:
the capital of Apathy is . . .

Sing-song: the song of scams:
Life burning in a lightbulb: (I am the light-switch-on)
Death swirling around a bowl: (I am the light-switch-off)

Too young to focus solely on such things I worry about the endless
government,
          mass extinction,
and the last gasp of gas in the Great Platonic
          Internal Combustion Engine called
          Man:

(Cup of the crystal sidewalk. Grail of teenage grails.)

End.
End of the scream,
sustained against all things: god, family, country, work, law,
          money, heartache, industry, boredom, invisible empires,
                    western philosophy, cataracts, masterpieces,
                    pop culture, dead time, fake blood, false teeth . . .

Capitulation of hope. Unconditional surrender of fantasy.

Down with the tyranny of love!
Power to the common distribution of dead-reality!

In the total absence of revolutionary fury, I still pray
            for the Glorious Reversal-of-Fortune:
            the wretched shall inherit the earth
            while the rich jump ship to the best seats in Heaven,
            season-ticket holders to the Fire Sale
                at Armageddon:

O O oh the song of scams:
this best-of-all-possible-worlds devours its young
while the smart sell debt to the bankrupt:

I am the light-switch-on:

outnumbered forever, I scream
for ice cream, I believe
I've seen everything there is to see:

Chicago crawling with buffalo,
the lost ruins of New York,
vines clutching the dead husks of D.C.,

I am an American dreaming.

MONEY MAN

I can travel forward in time. I just stand here and there I go.
The world is as old as I am but I don't equal the world. Hung
by my bloody gums over the exchange floor, I writhe and I
masturbate and piss reality: what a war the world is; how quickly
lords turn to loans. I can spread myself as thin as nothing
and there I go . . . becoming the map again. The spitting image of
not being. I'm the man made of money and no one can hear me
scream.

THERE IS NO EYE IN SEA

and so John wandered, bentbacked and buzzed from beer, drifting down through waves of snowfall, flakes of sky peeking out against the glowing dark, colliding and creeping down his blushdrunk cheek, a flashflood drifting through the waves of peachhair and bloodwarm skin, backbent down to the ends of his fingertips, coalescing into a tear, slipping off the bitten nail and plummeting then into the pavement, into the moaning dirt, the drop bursting, dancing, drifting down through the waves of grass and dead leaves, underneath the soles of sleepwalkers, down through the veins of the junkyard hills, and plummeting then into the Nashua River, into the crowd of snowmelt and mad sweat leapfrogging over each other and the earth, eating the rocks and the dirt, down, down, down, through cowtowns and milltowns and towns for the bosses, the Nashua becoming the Merrimack, the Merrimack becoming the sea, and falling finally, bentbacked and buzzed, into The Atlantic Ocean of Unemployed Blood, a breathing giant stroking the crotch of his motherwife, The Shore, in a seasick sleepsex song that a well read sonovabitch like John would like to call the History of Western Civilization (or Some Shit), a nightmarish and incomplete work of neurotic arrogance and immolating genius, an afterbirth miscarriage of biblical proportions, thousands of years of cultures and kids eating each other's carrion, and now in this turning year, now with everything coalescing and cumulating in the whitewash wavebreak of the eternal ladyfriend, the road becoming a tear, the Shore finally cumming, screaming, crying bloodymurder from her empty world-womb "Atlantic! Atlantic! O God O God Oh godgodgodgodgod!" so that the fault lines shivered with union labor and climax and a babe was born of this bored ache of the Word, shrieking, bawling, crying out "this is the song that never ends! this is the song that never ends! this is the song that never ends . . ." front lawns, frozen ground, a chained dog howling at No-One, drunk kids kissing behind an abandoned garage, and John, Johnny, Jonathan, Author of Revelations, drifting through the waves of terror running like seafoam snowmelt down the blushdrunk cheek of old wartorn Who-Am America, Mother Of Rivers, Mother of Orphans, and Mother of John Mother-fucker who was left here in Misery, Massachusetts amongst the ex-fathers and downsized blood, his muddy heart, a drop bursting, drifting down through the frozen ground, through the grass and dead leaves, underneath the disappointed streets, eating the road and the dirt and the decades between, down, down, down, searching for her, or Him, or Her, in hope of plummeting finally into that rumored sea but not even God escapes grammar and so John wandered

ART IS A HYMEN YAWNING

"Come clean!" The over-voice of the Void blooms
vomit. God's sea men siege / the womb waves / the white-
whale. Cup of the crystal sidewalk. Grail of teenage grails.
Shipwrecked animal, seized engine of flesh. O tense hips,
a wounded Word with you, please . . .

Art is a hymen yawning.

Come clean, the last Century was our Passion play: Jesus
fucking Christ chewed between the laissez-faire jaws of life.
Mother's milk kissed through the fangs of Her global capitalist
syster. Rome's hot teeth gnashing in the divine sewer. Our termite
civilization reclines: irrotic terror isms, blind king of the I.
Immaculate birth of the well-fed totalitariat.

I'm coming clean baby, *we're* the bad neighborhood. I am
soulsick. You swallow your sentences. I am bent nails. You are
what you eat. We screw in the eyes of the hammering crowd.
It's the Glory of Man . . . there's always a book in the assassin's
bag. A thick body of lit to keep the bulimic pigs fed. And we're so
well read.

PROJECT ETERNAL UNIVERSE

Project Eternal Universe
was doomed from the start.

That's what we've been learning in Catastrophe 204.
Our grad student is a wounded knee.
Our classroom is the dustbin of the Future.
We've been falling for decades
at thirty-two feet per second
towards the palpitating heart
of the heart of the country.

"Catastrophe," our grad student says, "is the dead risen
to bus tables, surf the web and wait again
for death. In a real catastrophe, it's always almost too late
and nobody knows it but
you. "

Father. Father.
Fatherland, I've been thinking about us as of late.
I've been thinking about our love and our hate
Together, and I'm thinking.
I thought a thought
and I'm thinking about
fear now. Father, I
know you
know me.
Please.

Project Eternal Universe is a Dream with a capital D,
a dandy lion lost in the suburbs,
gnashing its teeth.

Project Eternal Universe is the Holy Ghost
feeling Cassandra up
in a wildfire west of Los Alamos.

Project Eternal Universe is over and can
never be revived by
no one ever.

Sway with me, scholars.

Sway like anarchists hanging in the summer wind,
like tit-suckled babes in the last throes of freedom,
like the stomach-shot soldier spitting
human waste home
into the dust.

Sway, sway.
This way, this way.

Into the bleak mud,
time's books sink.
Our eye-oh-yous erased in rot and error.

Who last laughs?
Who holds court?
Who keeps score?

Who will read these poems when the people are gone?

Poor eyeless poor
resigned to death
and all for war. Every
art fag dead and God
still born.

The text is foolish. Falter, fraud.
Fuck. Fuck. Fuck it.
We've let go

Project Eternal 'verse
Project Eternal

Death has been banished by the destruction of all life
so He walks alone
searching for cigarettes.
Sex Ed

womb of worm
and towers twin
up all night with phantom limbs
trysts in trenches
flaccid lies
bit lip spin
sundered signs
surrendered borders
terror ties
who's fucked
and who's fucking?
it's the old in and out
again

U.S.

Heavy-set Satan on the black tar plain.
Heavy-set Satan on his private highway home.

We're gonna hang for our fathers;
sold souls on the road.

The dead are patient in the bedrock.
The dead whistle in the cold.

We're gonna hang for our fathers;
for their eyes and ours.

The past is paved on our Vegas mugs.
Elvis, ask your brother.

Who damns who
in self-made America?

Dollars crumpled like Appalachians.
Pyramids like pocket change like wastewater.

Vacuum of a nation
grinning with a mouthful of holes.

Who damns who?

The interstate is a dead end, charred crust—
a trophy to planned obsolescence.

The strip mall is a Venus-fly-trap.
The strip mall is a suicide pact between unborn panthers.

I am a spy, searching for a fatherland.
I go under covers to be born again.

Heaven-sent Satan in the Chamber of Commerce.
Overturning tables in a Temple of Doom.

The human heart is home alone.

U.S. and us.

POLITICS

Politics once inspired me but I'm through
dirty soap screamed the janitor's parade
Union of Disillusioned Idealists Local 213
all good cops go to heaven

WACHUSETT

O Wachusett!
O sleeping giant!
       belly fulla beer & ashes
       cumulus wisp of razors
O funeral star!
O pinkheaded evening!
Keep my love between your
       daughter's shut thighs
       & cellars
       dead heat hermaphrodite: June
(sky sun)

Get some shuteye
       cinder
       flooded valley / swollen river (bed, heartache, boneyard)
Get some sleep

O Wachusett!
O dead roads   hold my hand!
                oh
                my lord

Wholely ghost   hold my hope &
Rise! Daughter dream-in

eat your wages   devour your twin
illiterate carrion   confess your waxwings!

All Man hates a good truth
                    (& all Hell weeps for the kids):

O Wachusett!
O haunted hole!
      oh years   scattered like fathers!
      oh fathers   scattered like leaves!

Keep my blood between your
      sweat stained streets

Keep my heart beneath your
      conscious   streams
      fallen   leaves

The sins of the mountain
      bestowed upon the sea—

The children have lost their dreams
      our mouths are full of
         class war liquor
         & lack of sleep

Our hearts are homes
      we can never hope
      to own &
      oh   dead friends
         doomed vandals!

The cul-de-sacs will burn with perfect holy hate
      Oh but
words are cheap & the mind is
      a terrible thing
      to ache…

Daydream terror   drunk-pink star
      gale of lives
      real wages

Daddy long-legs

Sell her love
        less sleep—
(darkness is everywhere / deaf leviathan of the sired sea)
—sell her dreams

O Wachusett!
O stolen blue mouth!
        unearthed sun   come
                      wake me up
     & Rise!
     up from your cellars and sing

Call the leaves   back to the trees
                      back into their wounds
     back up the driveway
     & into the womb

O lost sleep!
O swollen pink   New England!
     I am a double agent ark-builder
     broken water
     difficult body
     of children's literature

I sail a stillborn sea:
     interstate run
     off

deaf valley

oh godless winter
oh worn soles
     dreamt heartache of dirty snow . . .

All Ages run home

— What do we want?
                Nothing!
— When do we want it?
                Now!

O Wachusett!
O ulcerate belly of stars!
             mountain of twilight / lake of fruit

O vulture's prey!
The whole world lies with perfect grace
             these grey hells / the bankrupt inferno!

Peace of waking sleep
             & children blown to bloody flakes
             along the poor streets of
             the universal
             daydream

O jobless lovers!
O setting suns   born unto trouble
             Burn your leaves & human hair:
             Stain the bad air
             with black smoke   ideal ape

Valley of Dreams
Eden crushed between tectonic sheets
             tread this ink blindly,
                          crushed toenails—
             make war on Gravity:

In exile the Old Moses Mountain sleeps
             with belly burning

& nightmares of hands
weeping on shuttered streets
             fathers
             long   gone
             calling us in / to the callous sea

O Wachusett!
O wet skin of my world!
        I am a heartworm:
I feed on your sedimental
        golden earth

My love is trapped in your snare of streets
        the dusty corners where
                no words reach
All the names I can't even speak

The dreams of girls buried
        under your dead leaves
        the rotting trash
                of the languid trees

The remains of years I chose to keep
        locked in code   in cold sweat
                sweet   dreams / stink
                of souls
                ripe   like lovers
                lying in the reeds

        spilled sleep   sixteen
        woke shivering   like screaming

seized   underneath a gray grave sea

O hole, what do you mean?
We, blank pages
            oh dying
        dream

O Wachusett!
> draw me under your waves
> into your buried world

Let me see the cellars of your stone heart
> the drowned wombs
> of your daughters

Let me wear dead King Phillip's
> crown of leaves

Let me carve my body in your tyrant's streets
O Bloody Soil!
O Teenage Sin!
I am your daughter dissolving in heat
I am your son setting in sleep

CLOSED FOREVER

(UNTITLED)

What kind of death have you saved for me?
A stuck fly against a white board
with my name engraved underneath?
I can't even write my name here.
It looks stupid against all this white space.
There is no corpse to line up.
It is like one of those places in the night sky
where even space is disappointed,
so I fill these empties with errors and
too many words. My mistakes
give me something to worry about
and that's fine. But I'd rather be able
to breathe this blank paper in
and out like air. That would be silence
whether or not I was
making a sound.

EXTINCTION BLUES

At the rapid end of the earth
where nothing happens
even nihilism loses its pleasures
even the wounds which pepper your face and hands like little
bulldozers come off as a billboard or a traffic report or
an advertisement to quit drinking,
> at best a warning to youth (wherever they might hide)
> that the middle class always wins.
And Literature will sound to you like an old woman coughing,
> out to breakfast with stubborn phlegm lodged in a cavern
> of cancer, half-convinced that behind the next hack lies freedom:
> the doom of the free.
Where the sun gets up just to get in your eyes
> and the century is a fist, a contusion, a debt paid in flesh . . .
where the blank depression of words trips you and you find a friend
> in your scars and declare squatter's rights on abandoned creation
> ghost-sick for God and a meaning
> behind the strip malls and rented rooms.
Failed revolutions, messiahs, fathers-on-tape, and the bookshelf bearing
> down on you like a paper tomb where dead voices slide
> their secrets into insomniac riddles, heart bloated with stale love
> at 3 AM with the computer mocking and a hundred thousand
> humans dreaming of work beside you.
At the rapid end of the earth
we'll be filthy rich on a dead planet
imprisoned in visions we chose to ignore.

REALITY GAS

Do you remember the parts of me?

My eyes: glass rivers slicing
canyons in the sun.

My legs: twin towers
choking on the succulent center of attention.

Laughing all the way to the bank,
the pigs feed on the bonepulp of their parents.
Chew chew chew
spit spit spit

I am here already.
Yes, it is time.

The children have all gone down the drain
and into the pipes.

The sewers are our solace.
The sweet and sour soup.

We bathe in the dead.
We drink to our youth.

There is no world left in the world
and even God lacks God.

Who holds court?
Who keeps score?
Who last laughs?
Reality gas!
Reality gas!
Reality gas!

ODE TO VIOLENCE

We have chewed our pens back to swords . . .

The art of words hath been given a shot
but having given its best,
it turned the heart on itself.

With every university stacked against us,
literature turns to garbage, litter
becomes currency, and cash
remains the practical
consolidation
of death.

Civilization conquers culture.
Empire devours art.

Half the Kids got tenure
and the other half got shot.

I refuse to write in the vague and clever sadness
        of my contemporaries; no,
my sadness will be the slobbering and bloodthirsty sadness of lovers
        like a car bomb or Juliet, the Communard
falling on her pen at the end of the line.

(UNTITLED)

Pain pours
from the mouths of people.

Every morning:

rocks of tooth rolling
mourning;
time's spine: jibber-jabber.

Pain pours
out the fingertips: a
machine that turns water to piss

a miracle
that can't count,

black roots: rainbow toes.

Godless pain
in the blue morning light:

time rolls downhill,
pain pours

a playful ocean,

in love

with love.

TIMES NEW ROMAN

All autumn we waited for the war to end.

We kept ourselves occupied
(paralysis, hysteria, canons made of bone)

as the damage collected with interest
on our doorsteps.

Each morning when I read the paper
I pulled a tooth that had gone bad overnight.

Rotted from the inside out,
I tore it from my mouth

like a rich harvest or a Caesar
appointing his heir.

I postmarked the incisors to my senator
and he sent me thousands upon thousands of dollars

for toothpaste, dental work, and floss
strung from gold;

I asked him,
"What have I done to deserve such love?"

And he laughed like a matador with a tongue made of flags.

We poets, who spit in our sleep
are only a dream of the homeland.

We are an incinerator's conscience
speaking in smoke and ashes.

We are the last nail, the final straw.
We drive the getaway car while we mourn

The dead to keep them quiet.

WHAT AILS US
AND WHAT TO DO ABOUT IT

All that is solid melts to air
—**Karl Marx**

How can one speak of the timeless in a time which denies time?
How can one speak at all
    if speaking is an act of duration
    that implies that one must not be interrupted by the cops
    or by the absolute censor which is Babel:
        not the Tower but the Market:
            the mean conduit of all communication?

And how can one adequately express the experience of empathy
    when the age is a gang rape masquerading as a formal dance,
    when to admit even the possibility that each human being is
        an irreplaceably precious thing
    implies a religious horror:
        a horror which addresses civilization itself
            as a factory which produces pavement
                and runs on the flesh of living things?

The artists, the poets, the musicians, and the mystics
    have been left with very little room to breathe.
They crowd and crush each other, the living trample the dead
    clawing at the doors of this burning brothel.
Their creations peck and claw each other
    and bring fuel and pretty lights to the fire
    which is the debt-driven exponential conversion
        of living earth to dead world.
Those closest to the exits
    may realize the doors are locked

may understand the crowd must turn around
        and charge the flames, despite the danger of
            pains not yet understood
                    by those outside industry of pain;
the crowd, however, pushes on . . .
        "To the exits!" they say:
                "They can't burn Nothing!"
                "Nothing won't burn!"

ANARCHIST MALL

Permit me love. Crackhouse,
car payment. Permit me
love. Amnesiac news. Permit
knowledge, paper heart.
Prop up the anorexic spirit
of the century, Christ-
Kross, killer beez,
amber-alert, rhetoric
fridgerator: "do not care.
do not care. do not care.
do not care." Super-
highway, where is
haunted hope? The divine
mystery of television. Lovers
propped up by
power lines. Crucifix,
highway home,
torture jewelry.
No one is cooler
than anyone else,
not even Proust.
Pain is endless.
Hope is a noose.
People everywhere,
do what thou wilt.

MOUNT EERIE

The starlight shining through broken teeth,
cracked jaws, and ribs.
The silver din of life rolling along
the bottom of the world.
All the sky above stirring in its sleep,
tossing the sheets of rain.
Sky sweating through the night
of an unlit home.
Deep space, the living room:
What does the furniture
talk about after we're
not around? Does it
argue about God?
Does a bookshelf
love its splinters
or envy them?
Do beds believe
in ghosts?
I believe
they
do.

NEW JERUSALEM

You can't try so hard not to be haunted:
in lost evenings, the trapdoors between words,
nerve-endings, ghost-flowers, never-ending happiness;

the whole deep-mythology of suburbia—
steady jobs in the day-to-day reproduction of death:
at the right hand of the Father, a haunted house Kingdom of God.

In between breaths, in door-mouths: the smashed glass eyes,
dead family in photographs staring right through you
like that's where the killer is.

You can't try so hard not to be haunted, Moloch,
my reader, my neighbor in Hell—
You can't try so hard to be real,

to be spontaneously sad and of the earth—
Not corpse paint, not folk rock, not pot leaf lightning
in the high definition war of all against all;

Moloch, bobbing for terrorists in Boston Harbor
with cash money on the radio
and the oil on fire on the black ceiling of the sea.

The carbon from Christ's cross is in your ashtray,
in your lower canines, in the D.C. pentagram, in your bloodstream
pushing past clotted cattle fat without saying "Sorry!" or
"Blessed are the poor"

I won't apologize for this shit I write.
I won't apologize for being afraid.
Punk rock changed my life and so did money.

The world is loaded.
Our dread moves mountains.
The New Jerusalem failed because of you and me.

HEART CRANE

I work on this fly trap of time.
Like the yawning fangs at the bottom of the workweek.
The clock's plot on the life of the President.
Because it's got one.
Kids plowing into one another w/ sick blood.
Repetitive motion, perpetual war.
The conversation money has with itself called a country.
Funny that.
I work on this.
I work on the family drama of love versus speed and time is money.
Power is still power is still power still.
Work on this open sore for sure w/ the ocean humming "Rape!"
    w/ the unquestioned victor of the 20th Century
    w/ the strength of 400 men working 40 hours
    w/ the explosive ejaculation of hours over the uncreated spread
    w/ world war four wanted dead or alive
    w/ out oars
Work on this heavy gravity.
Jars of puke.
Feet of concrete.
In the outer space between extinction and prebirth,
every finger on the button,
I make ends meet.

I work on this.
I drink death straight.
What memories do you have left?
      From pumping gas?
      From sitting between the gutter and the stars?

THE KINGDOM OF HEAVEN

1.

The falling sun fills in the day. Day-drops
on the eyes of interest. Dreamers lay fallow, stuck on
the clock, their wheels spin on dark matter. They starve
under sheets looking for holes in nothing, be nothing be
no thing be

I sleep with my eyes unlocked to thieves
while the work week feeds
on losses and tabletops, on the bland things in things:
divorce courts, a yacht for Ulysses,
with all the lights on
and all my heroes made of carbon
and the black oil on fire on top of the sea.

Akimbo resurrection of the sun, I observe with
piss libation and sacramental coffee.
Monday morning the clever gather to worship
the holy mystery of money
while the rest are crushed into capital-feed.

O Golgotha!
O shipwrecked children of colleges!
O Tuesday spent drowning in memories!
O unremarkable History!

Lost Lord, save us from words
which make us thirst,
save us from the seductive hatred
of happiness.

We twist in the anonymous fires of we.

2.

Start with you and everyone you know will be dead very soon.
Start with that.
Start with the big-picture pointlessness of all activity.

Money which flows through us like divine love.
Money like a man tied to the tide
Money, my love, my hope, my good life.
Money, hold me lover and sing.

Haunted houses on every street.
Crooked family trees
        burning bush / fallen leaves
the girls underneath
        swollen with hopes
        sloshing over the shore and back again
                in the earth-pot dreaming.

Start with the brokenhearted nature of anywhere
        where girls and boys congregate and disappear
        where hopes and things collide and charm

and beg each other for death, to come back
to the oceanic dirt
the system of energy
crossing light-years of nothing
        gas-stove universe
                of conscious streams
the green fuse that drives
my used heart
to work and back:

for new children, new loves, new presidents made of corn syrup and
the deep mysteries of suburbia,
the graves of bacteria,
the relics of black metal teens,
        utopian bomb-throwing VFW terror-tantrums
        moshing to victory.

And I don't feel 23
I don't feel anything.
Isn't it funny?

Start with omnipotent sympathy.
Start with an echoing love,
        ghost flowers
        echoing New England purity
        dead trees
        the putrid valentine of History
        coming between your knees
                (A screaming. A trophy.)

Start with the superhighway to hell
        and Christ on the radio
        rocking out with your favorite stars.
                (Sirus, Alpha Centurti, the North Magnetic Cloud)

Start with the dead seas
        and the wastelands of America
        and the rotting carcass of life on Earth
        begging
        for a better mousetrap.

3.

All the libraries mean nothing.
All the slaughterhouses.
All the mansions built by fear
will burn to the earth, will cower under religious lightning.

The old debts of kings
to their kingdom
will be paid in full.

The strip malls are thirsty with young pain,
a loneliness made of youth.

I will be thrown out with the daily news.
I will be the refuse of debris.
I will touch my heart with pliers and strip every screw
          and open it up to reveal the crusty oil and birthday cards
                    stuck in the cracks.
Hold my hand, holy girlfriend.
Death is a breath away and made of doubt,
                    which is the earnest awe of all things for all things.

Death is certain and imminent.
No healthier philosophy exists to spirit human beings
toward their most beautiful dreams.

My religion is made of love
          not for the abstract
          but the concrete enjoyment of experience.

My love is a wisp of dirt
          in a black box
          and soon I will be.

The Kingdom of Heaven in the soles of your feet.

THE GLORY OF MAN

We write our dictionaries in blood and piss.
("Keep it fucking down!")
I'm quietly quitting
cuz the TV's too loud
and I'm drowning out
in the ether,
huffing paper cuts
and hearing AIDS
shouting loud:
"What a fucking cop-out!"
What a great deal
what a natural disaster,
the cops are the real killers
and I'm outing this quiet
for all our childrens' children's
futures.
Hey, humanist,
please shut the fuck up,
this is my shout out
and there's so many people I'd like to thank:
My teachers, my habits,
God, Dad,
goddamnit.
We're only killing time
between infinite quiets
(two world wars and a sludge of afterbirth).
It's the Glory of Man:
there's always a book in the killer's bag
a thick body of Literature
to keep the bulimic pigs fed
and I'm so well-read
I'm so well-read.

LETTERBOMB #2

Dear Sir or Madam,

I wrote this letter in the belly of a universe: at the exact moment of your birth, you pulled one of six billion names from the ontological hat and now here you are: a ticking timebomb in the mailbox of No-One: a lifespan moving money between agendas like an aqueduct: the Party of God, the pleasure centers of the skull hijacked by 2,000 years of idea-demons, the spell of words: an American citizen with balls full of radioactive cum and a master's degree in the dominant illusions of the century.

(The King was traditionally buried with objects He may need in the afterlife: an American Express card, a good lawyer, letters of reference, biological weapons, coupons, 401K, the True Cross, etc.)

What is the meaning of evil? A door that believes in the wall.

*

GIRL

Girl,
I've been singing for you
for so long, it's almost
sin. Our coffins are calling,
so come on, twist
and shout. Hell, I've been
waiting for you my whole life
so come closer, I
hold all fear and lonely doubt
in my hand like a kitten. Come,
come, stay soft
sweet singing
girl.

DEBT COLLECTION AGENCY

Tragic flaw: love for us. Cross-bearer,
come down from your cloud. I say "sum"
and the whole hole echoes: scum. Sorry, star.
When the sun of Man burns out
who'll pay the national debt?

The machines have come to life
but instead of political power, they
are begging for death.

The middle class is eating the future to feed the past.
You have History and I have mine.

All doom / held like lilacs / in the center of the eye /
in the slip of the tongue /
in the cauldron of the Heart / what's cookin / good lookin?

ADVICE FOR THE YOUNG

Blood. Blued.
Body in water.
A backyard of dreams.
Say nothing.
Scream the hum of ah.
Consider god
as a coughing fit, if the coffin fits.
Leak of joy.
Careless ash to ashes.
Every war criminal has a first love.

Consider god
       as a landfill
       as paper-machete
       as a bull in a china shop
       as a thermometer
       an unpublished poet
       a meaningless question
       a paperweight
       a coin toss
       a private i
       a locked door
       as a mean drunk
       a blind librarian
       a stone
       a stain on the sheets
       as the ringing in your ears
       as a grad student without hope
       the corner of her mouth
       her hair
       her bite
       as time
       as a hole . . . as a hole . . . as a hole . . . as a hole . . . .

Dropping prayers like breadcrumbs
on the long road
into the world.

The whole horror laid out
like a nude on a blanket
come hithering with a mouth full of flies.

The Psalms of Boredom.
The Psalms of Convenience.
The Psalms of In-Flight Entertainment

These are our blues.

These are the songs of the underground hogs
at the last supper of
King Swine.

The desert is Death
one by lonely
one

until the tides come in
and wash the wake
away.

Love,
rabid and whole
is our only defense.

I hope you know how to hate, lions.